A souvenir guide

Barrington Court
Somerset

Katherine Lambert

National Trust

History in the Heart of Somerset

In the village of Barrington, which stands on the edge of the Somerset levels, an unobtrusive entrance leads down to the mansion, cottages and farm buildings of the Barrington estate.

There has been a house on the site since Domesday, and for five centuries after the Norman Conquest Barrington Court was in the hands of a branch of the Daubeney family. Their mixed fortunes were typical of the period. Sir Ralph and Sir Philip died in the Crusades; Sir Giles, stripped of his lands by Richard III, rose under Henry VII to Lord Chamberlain. His son Henry was arrogant enough to parade 80 of his servants and horses through the streets of London; although he was ennobled as the Earl of

Above The Court's irregular plan gives character and movement to the south front

Right The Tudor house in 1920: a ruin on the road to restoration

continuing existence are all rooted in trade. It was William Clifton, a London merchant, who built the Court, completing it around 1560. William Strode, a clothier from Shepton Mallet, 'bestowed money and labour to restore the Court to its pristine beauty' after 1633. In 1674 Strode's son, also named William, erected a grandiose stable block now known as Strode House. In the 20th century it was Colonel Arthur Lyle, a sugar magnate from Amersham, who from 1919 made the house and estate what it is today.

Restoration and reinvention

It nearly didn't happen: during the 19th century the Court had been reduced to the status of a tenanted farmhouse and in parts was virtually a ruin. In 1907, however, it was bought by Julia Woodward of Clevedon, who gifted it to the National Trust as one of its earliest acquisitions. With no endowment and a seemingly bottomless restoration budget needed, it was a potential white elephant of enormous size. Colonel Lyle's offer to restore the property in return for a 99-year lease was providential indeed.

It was the start of a compelling chapter in the history of Barrington Court as a trio of strong-minded individuals came together: the patron Arthur Lyle, the architect James Edwin (J.E.) Forbes, and the garden designer Gertrude Jekyll. Working out who suggested what, which recommendations were heeded and which

Bridgewater in 1538, he lost his status and fortune after his marriage to Lady Katherine Howard, aunt of Henry VIII's unfortunate fifth wife. The Daubeneys' Barrington connection was finally severed when a cousin, Sir Thomas Arundel of Lanherne, was executed for treason in 1552.

Rooted in trade

Significantly, the estate's architectural grandeur, periods of stability and prosperity, and

ignored, and which pieces of the jigsaw the National Trust has decided to keep and promote in the future, is a great part of the fascination of the place.

The Lyles

Just two months after being invalided home from the Battle of Aubers Ridge in May 1915, Arthur Lyle and his wife Elsie first set their eyes, and their sights, on Barrington.

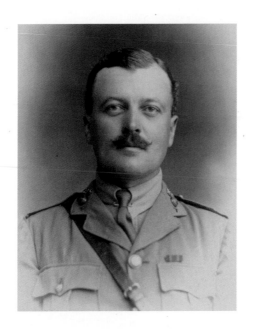

He ended his army career as Honorary Colonel of 10th Battalion, the London Regiment in 1921 to concentrate on his new life in Somerset, having resigned from the family firm of Lyle and Sons when it became Tate & Lyle. It's an indication of both his wealth and his enthusiasm that when he took on the Barrington lease he was willing and able to put £100,000 of his own money into a place that he would never own.

A family affair
Arthur's son Ian and grandson Andrew followed in his footsteps, both at Tate & Lyle and at their beloved Barrington. They were three of a kind – generous, entertaining and approachable. Sir Ian, knighted in 1959 for 'services to sugar', was a notably brave and resourceful naval commander

Above Arthur Abram Lyle in 1914, 1st City of London Regiment Royal Fusiliers

Left and right Lyle's golden syrup, the family firm's most famous product – iconic in shape, style and slogan

with an endearing touch of British eccentricity. On one occasion he joined a madcap scheme for racing cheetahs and on another he welcomed a new officer at Newhaven railway station wearing a Persian rug, with a tin hat and a gas mask for a sporran, 'singing a rather vulgar Scottish song and making a horrid piping noise' with an improvised set of bagpipes.

Kin and community

As employers, the Lyles trod the fine line between being caring towards their people and remaining conscious of their standing in the local community – caps were doffed, but many a good party was hosted at the Court. The Colonel's vision, embracing as it did not only the newly created estate but also the existing village, gave him responsibilities that were wider than many landowners'. He and wife Elsie (most often known as Ronnie) embraced their roles with gusto. Land was given for allotments west of the village, lighting and heating supplied to the church, and a cricket pitch laid out. Local groups and societies were invited to gather together at the Court, and on Fridays the children were invited in to listen to nature talks on the village's

Above Ian Lyle at Hartley Wintney with a friend's racing cheetah

one and only radio. Christmas was heralded by a party with a giant tree and presents for all the children, though the fascinating draw was the flamboyantly coloured Amazonian parrot making its ceremonial entrance down the main staircase on the Colonel's shoulder. George VI's Coronation in 1937 was celebrated by a tea party with games for the children and a mug for all. 'Polly Parrah' kept order on her stand and balloons were released to float over the ha-ha.

The magic worked both ways. As a child Andrew Lyle remembers idyllic summer evenings in his bedroom overlooking the Lily Garden: 'We were sent to bed fairly early, and you could hear the fountains on the water in the pond, and the swallows, and the wood pigeon that always seemed to nest in the magnolia on the wall. And you'd also hear the very polite clapping coming from the direction of the cricket field, and the sound of leather on willow was really very good indeed.'

ABRAM LYLE & SONS Limited

OUT OF THE STRONG CAME FORTH SWEETNESS.

SUGAR REFINERS.

The Court

The Court has been described by the eminent architectural historian, Christopher Hussey, as 'the final and most free expression of pure Gothic design as applied to secular buildings'.

Originally thought to have been commissioned by the Earl of Bridgewater c.1514, the Court has now been dated almost fifty years later, to the start of the age of Elizabeth I. Because of the need to fit a great hall, screens passage, pantry and buttery into the ground floor, the unusual E-shaped plan is not completely symmetrical. Contemporary with Poundisford, Brympton and Mapperton, a group of local houses with remarkably similar features and dates, it's a marvellous marriage of mellow hamstone, clean and emphatic vertical lines and fantastical rooftop ornamentation.

The relatively plain north façade at the rear of the house was to become Colonel Lyle's new entrance front, facing the buildings of his model estate. The south façade, which was the original entrance, looked out across lawn to pastureland sloping gently up towards a horizon of wooded hills. In 1560 the newly erected mansion, dignified by a setting of grandiose formal gardens, would have dominated the scene entirely without any competition from the adjacent red-brick stable block built a century later. Now the two, tethered together by a narrow brick corridor, are moored in a sea of green. It is the potent presence of these buildings in the landscape that makes the most immediate impact and remains one of the most enduring memories of a visit to Barrington.

A tale of two houses

Ironically, William Clifton's pure Gothic vision was irrevocably eroded by two key decisions made by Arthur Lyle, a passionate amateur antiquarian. When he took the lease, he was determined to let the architecture of the Court speak for itself. He therefore significantly reduced the ambitious landscaping and planting schemes proposed by his architect, J. E. Forbes. He also decided to convert the 17th-century Strode building – then a stable block housing a

Top Strode House and the Court – an unexpected architectural pairing

Above Barleytwist chimneys add a final flourish to the Court's roofline

dozen horses and two coaches – into the family's main abode. In the process he squared off the U-shaped building, creating a courtyard garden and turning the stables into a handsome red-brick box that is almost as imposing in its way as the mansion it once served. As it turned out, Strode House did not become the Lyles' sole family home. They lived at the Court intermittently after its completion in 1925 until the Second World War, and Sir Ian moved back there again in 1962 after the early death of his beautiful wife, Julia.

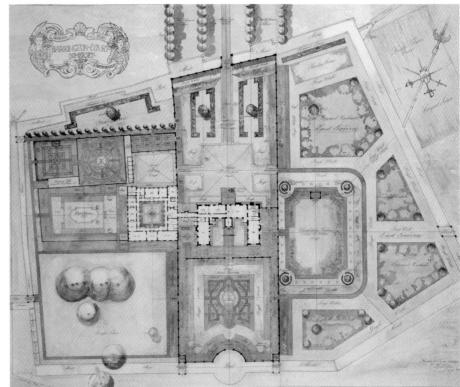

Right J. E. Forbes' plan, exquisitely drawn and painted in 1917, would have surrounded the two houses with formal gardens arranged in a complicated geometric layout that was positively Elizabethan in its scale and ambition. In the event, only the five acres on the west side of Strode House were carried out

Ground Floor

Over the centuries the English country house has played many roles, as retreat, power base, dynastic showcase. Arthur Lyle's main reason for taking over the Court, and its most immediate impact today, was none of these: it was to house an important collection of woodwork salvaged from derelict buildings up and down the country.

A passion for collecting

In just a few years before the outbreak of the First World War Lyle sought out, dismantled and stored not only yards of oak panelling but entire rooms. It took two carpenters and a labourer, working under his strict supervision, three years to fit all his finds into their new surroundings. The grandest pieces were reserved for the ground floor. The family's Small Dining Room was singled out by Nikolaus Pevsner for its elaborate star-patterned ceiling and spectacular early-16th-century screen rescued, it is thought, from the Bishop's Palace at Gaywood in Norfolk. The Great Hall has a range of fine linenfold panelling, including panels of French parchemin, a simple version of the linenfold style, on the backs of the double doors.

Contemporary photographs and the catalogue drawn up when the contents were sold in 1978 show that the Court was also richly furnished. The rooms were filled with handsome Jacobean furniture, Eastern carpets and rugs, fine porcelain and Oriental ceramics, tin-glazed earthenware, pewter and metalwork – and the animal skins which were in fashion in the 1920s and 30s. The house then stood empty until 1986, when it was sublet to Stuart Interiors, who used

Left French parchemin panels on the back of the doors of the Great Hall

Above The Old Kitchen c.1970s with its enormous Tudor fireplace

Right The Tudor Buttery c.1970s. It was richly panelled after its 1923 restoration

it as a showroom for antique and reproduction furniture and textiles. Andrew Lyle, the Colonel's grandson, surrendered the lease back to the Trust in 1991.

A home for owls

During its decades as a farmhouse in the late 19th century, however, the story was very different. J.E. Forbes' sister-in-law recorded that in the west wing (the only part still occupied), 'walls and panelling were covered with a sickly green paint, lace curtains draped the windows and not a single stick of furniture was suitable for its setting'. During the Easter holidays of 1921, Forbes, the Colonel and 14-year-old Ian ripped out five fireplaces of different periods concealing the huge original hearth of the Old Kitchen. Windows had been boarded up, panelling and fittings destroyed; it was possible to stand in the cellar and look straight up into the roof. Cider kegs were kept in the master's parlour, and owls hooted and pattered mournfully through the Long Gallery.

An artisan approach

Today, soundly restored, the Court is empty once again, preserved by the National Trust as an atmospheric shell encrusted with oak panelling and spiral staircases, fireplaces and floor slabs, studded walls and timbered ceilings. Arthur Lyle chose as his architect and landscaper J.E. Forbes, who had worked for him at Beel House in Buckinghamshire. It was a serendipitous choice: Forbes' sensitive and scholarly approach during the 1919–25 refit ensured a seamless blending of work by different hands, carried out in different ages. The Stair Hall is an example of this in a small space. The timbered ceiling came from a house in Hereford, the staircase originated in a Scottish castle, and the circular wrought-iron electrolier, a chandelier with electric lights, was made by Singers in nearby Frome. Although it may at first seem alien to wander through a network of largely bare rooms and corridors, without the distraction of furnishings the innate strength and spatial grace of the Court's internal architecture shines through.

In Tudor country houses, the needs of the owner's family and public life and the servicing of them went hand in hand. The master's parlour, which is now the Library, and the Great Hall were

Left Singers' electrolier framed by the Scottish staircase

Above A mirror-holding monkey carved on the north entrance door asserts the vanity of man

linked by a screens passage to the Buttery, the provision store for liquor and perishable foods. Beyond the passage lay the Old Kitchen with its huge fireplace and turnspit, which served as a brewhouse, bakehouse, smokery and salting room. The Gaywood screen itself was the Tudor equivalent of the Victorian green baize door: a decisive barrier between the west and east wings. So when the Lyles created their Small Dining Room in the 'elbow' of the Buttery and the Kitchen, they were dislocating a long-standing architectural tradition.

The Great Hall

In the Great Hall, the minstrel's gallery is a reminder of the plays, masques and musical entertainments that took place at Barrington in the Tudor period. The cleverly engineered sprung dance floor known as the 'Valtor' laid by Arthur Lyle in the Great Hall is the modern equivalent; a handle for adjusting its tension is located in the Stair Hall next door. These two public rooms came into their own again in 1925, when Arthur and Elsie Lyle welcomed 200 guests to an inaugural ball that continued until dawn.

Many of the early gatherings at Barrington Court were political. While William Strode II was Member of Parliament for Ilchester in 1679, he wooed his supporters 'with his great treats in the town and large invitations of his party to his house in Barrington'. The following year, rather more dangerously, he entertained the Duke of Monmouth, who in 1685 was to suffer a crushing defeat at the Battle of Sedgemoor seven miles to the north. A medallion struck with Monmouth's head was found under paving in the master's parlour. Strode's friendship with a pretender to the English throne cost him rather dear: he was fined £1500 and was lucky to escape with his life.

Lights! Camera! Action!
Barrington is well used to being taken over by film crews. The Great Hall, the Buttery, Joan Lyle's Bedroom and the Master Bedroom all featured in the darkly atmospheric 2015 television series, *Wolf Hall*. Although Hilary Mantel's story is set in the first half of the 16th century, when the aristocratic Daubeneys lived at Barrington, it was the self-made and politically astute William Clifton who seems closest to her anti-hero, Thomas Cromwell.

In the medieval and Tudor periods the public rooms were not confined to the ground floor.

The Master Bedroom and the Solomon Room

The great chamber, now the Master Bedroom, immediately above the Master's Parlour, reached by a spiral staircase in the small angle tower adjoining the Great Hall, was used for dining and gaming as well as sleeping. Its equivalent in the west wing, the Solomon Room, was possibly the original court house for trying manorial or ecclesiastical cases. It is accessed, together with the first-floor bedrooms, via Forbes' fine modern staircase fitted into the old south-west stairwell (see right).

These rooms yield a tantalising glimpse of the scale and quality of the 17th-century interiors. The overmantel of the hamstone fireplace in the great chamber celebrates the marriage in 1621 of the 32-year-old William Strode I to Joan Barnard,

Above Elsie Lyle's beloved Delft tiles pattern the bathroom separating the bedrooms of her daughter Joan and son Ian

Above right Now bereft of its bright colours the 17th-century *Judgement of Solomon* overmantel in the Strode Bedroom

a wealthy heiress aged 14. It's an elaborate, originally highly coloured affair, where the central coat of arms is flanked by a pair of panels decorated with interlacing strapwork bands. In the Solomon Room the plaster overmantel of the same date illustrates a biblical dilemma and is framed by a bold strapwork cartouche.

A family home

Under the Lyles, all the first-floor rooms were used as bedrooms. The generous Tudor windows, impressive fireplaces and the timber studding sit alongside the usual trappings of an early-20th-century domestic interior. Indoor plumbing provided hot water for baths, and replaced the ubiquitous commode; illumination came in the shape of Art Nouveau light fittings, sconces and electroliers.

Here too the carpenter's carving skills and patching skills of Arthur Lyle were called on. In the Strode Bedroom they reassembled 17th-century pine panelling collected from another room in the house, while an unusual design featuring the St Andrew's cross was installed in Ian Lyle's Bedroom; the adjoining bathroom, as others on this floor, have Delft tiles cut by Elsie Lyle using 'old Dutch tiles bought from Belgium for the backs of the baths and basins' ('Granny made the most fiendish jigsaws', recalled her grandson Andrew).

Intricate stairways
When the Lyles arrived, they could see right up to the roof. The craftsmanship and Forbes' imaginative sense of design is shown in his staircase. Leading up to the Long Gallery, it may have been inspired by the barleytwist detailing on the Elizabethan chimneys visible outside the windows.

Second Floor

The Court's attic storey was virtually untouched when Forbes took over; it was also virtually roofless.

When Canon Hardwicke Rawnsley, one of the founders of the National Trust, visited it on an intelligence-gathering mission after reputedly downing a flagon of the strong local cider, he found the attics open to the elements and full of owls, which 'make a noise at night as if people were shuffling about and dragging weights over the rough boarding'. In spite of this he was won over by the light and grace of the building, urging the Trust to adopt it as part of its nascent portfolio.

The Long Gallery

The Long Gallery, covers the entire roof area with shorter corridors piercing into the gables, and is a rare survivor from the 16th century. When rain prevented them from exercising outside, it was a favourite place for the Tudor ladies of the house to stroll, their gossiping and games of battledore and shuttlecock sometimes interrupted by the gentlemen perfecting their swordplay. Heated by a handsome hamstone fireplace, small rooms lead off, lit by dormer windows giving fine views over the garden and the surrounding countryside. It's also a chance to see at close quarters the dramatic spiral chimneys finished by finials decorated with intricate scale-work caps.

Within the gallery are structural posts inserted in the 1920s and decorated with 17th-century marquetry depicting mortality and the passing of time: a skull and crossbones, the

tree of life, the grim reaper's scythe, the executioner's block and axe, an hour glass and a sundial, and possibly a depiction of Charles I. Curious details, rather creepy by comparison with the poignant piece of 17th-century graffiti painstakingly carved on the embrasure of the end window in the eastern arm of the gallery: the name of Johanna, youngest daughter of William Strode.

Above left and above **The Long Gallery, before (1916) and after restoration**

Left and right **Details of the naïve marquetry designs inlaid into structural posts. One set is dated 1670**

The Strodes and the Cliftons

Two Williams – Clifton the original builder and Strode the first restorer – were the prime architects of Barrington Court. The Cliftons' ownership of the house ended in 1605, with the suicide of Gervase Clifton, imprisoned for debt in the Fleet; his son had previously been mauled at a bear-baiting contest, and later died from his injuries. The Strodes' era was a happier one. William I was a wealthy and much loved local benefactor. Having turned down the honour of being made an Alderman in the City of London, he died at Barrington in 1666, leaving his fortune to the surviving nine of his 16 children. The line terminated with the death of the childless William Strode III c.1745.

Lyle's Vision & Model Estate

At Barrington, in Christopher Hussey's view, 'the bringing of a village *to* a mansion and the formation of the mediæval institution of a manor place, in social and architectural relation to a great house, is probably unique'.

It's the exact opposite of the centuries-old tradition of communities clotting together, for employment or self-protection, around the central hub of a castle, manor or abbey. On that first seminal visit in 1915, the Lyles came upon a property that was run down, ransacked, on the verge of ruin. Farm buildings pressed against the northern face of the Court, and cowsheds, pigsties and a manure pit were its pungent neighbours. Having added to the original 206 acres, acquiring farms and building up a herd of prize-winning Guernseys, the family endowed it with a sizeable landholding.

A grand scheme

For a place which exudes order, calm and space, the layout designed by J. E. Forbes in close consultation with the Lyles was unexpectedly complex. The approach, to the west of the row of six thatched cottages, was planned to lead between two imposing lodges at the beginning of a tree-lined avenue, and the workaday buildings – barns, animal sheds, motor house, garages and laundry – were set around tarmacked quadrangles at either side of the present access road. The re-siting of the Court's entrance to the north front was just one element in a grand scheme in which the two mansions were anchored by a cruciform pattern of arrow-straight roads, lined by formal avenues, with farm houses at the end of their axes. The main horticultural interest, confined to the Kitchen Garden and the formal gardens famously influenced by Gertrude Jekyll, was

Rest and recreation

There are no follies at Barrington, but a lighter-hearted side of the estate architecture is revealed by a series of ancillary buildings. When Streete Court School, founded in 1894 by the father of A. A. Milne, was evacuated from Westgate-on-Sea to Barrington at the start of the Second World War, a troupe of muddy and enthusiastic boys would follow the Barrington Beagles, a pack which was housed in kennels originally envisaged as a model railway shed. The roof of the cricket pavilion is stylishly thatched, and the Kitchen Garden is overlooked by an intriguing two-storey cottage purpose-built as a racquets court.

hidden behind walls and not immediately visible. The overriding importance of the model estate in the Colonel's scheme of things was thus made abundantly clear.

The overall interest of the site rests as much with the finely judged distribution of the many buildings in the landscape as it does with the gardens and features that adorn it. Vistas, ratios and distances were all carefully planned, and Forbes, whose talents lay not only in details but in the big picture, made good use of the existing character of the landscape. To appreciate this, walk from the main drive on the north side of the house up to the line of Court Cottages, then look back towards the workshops, taking in not only the austere north front of the Court and the huddle of farm buildings, but the meadows, the orchards, the double avenues of tulip trees and the ground rising gently towards the horizon behind.

Above A sycamore stands between the moat and the racquets court positioned in the south-east corner of the Kitchen Garden

Above left View towards Strode House and the Court post restoration c.1930s

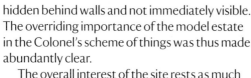

Left The stock yard, post restoration c.1925

The Gardens

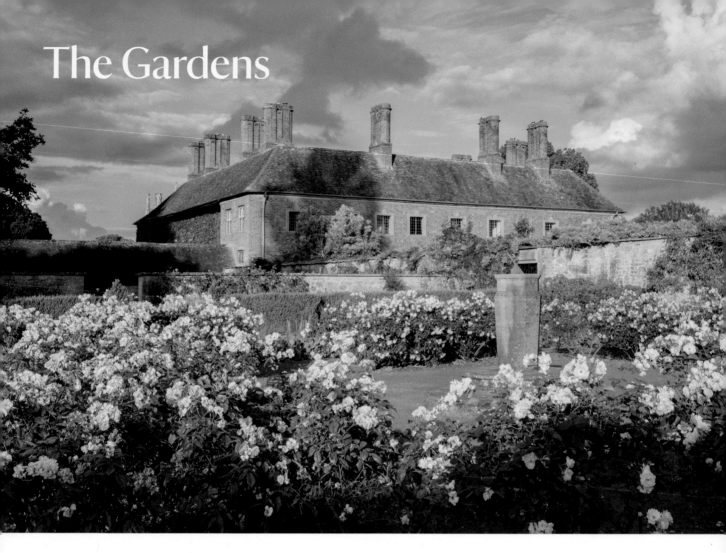

The enclosed formal gardens surrounding Strode House, occupying the site of an old farmyard, are just a small part of the 15-acre mosaic of gardens on the 1917 plan with which J.E. Forbes intended to embellish the Court and Strode House.

The Lily Garden

The largest of the three and the first to be planted, the Lily Garden remains closest of all to Gertrude Jekyll's executed designs for Barrington Court. Her wish-list of plants, famously selected after biscuit tins of Barrington's soil were sent to her in Munstead Wood, was worked into a scheme by Forbes and Elsie Lyle in 1924 and has been further refined by the National Trust in the Jekyllian spirit.

The architectural elements – Strode House's mellow red-brick walls, the large waterlily pond

Above left The Rose and Iris Garden, its central sundial surrounded by formal beds of English hybrid musk roses

Above from top Rosa 'Buff Beauty'; R. 'Felicia'; the bearded iris 'Wedgwood'

Right A rare survivor among vernacular farm buildings, the Grade-II-listed Buss Stalls were preserved by Colonel Lyle

set in grass, the quarry-tiled terrace and decoratively patterned paths – provide the strong framework needed for a rich and changing planting scheme. Bold and dark-foliaged shrubs set against the 10-foot walls on three sides of the garden act as foils for the flower borders, and the walls themselves are festooned with climbers. The planting follows Jekyll's rainbow spectrum, with an intricate combination of fine detail and bold sweeps of colour: orange, scarlet and crimson near the house, pink and white circling the central beds, yellows catching the eye at the far end. The tide of colour washes irresistibly into the centre of the garden: in two of the raised beds, the main impact comes from 12 different varieties of Knaphill azalea; the other pair is dramatically planted with dark-red 'Grenadier' dahlias.

In her influential *Colour in the Flower Garden*, first published in 1908 with later editions entitled *Colour Schemes for the Flower Garden*, Jekyll advocated devoting 'certain borders to certain times of year; each border or garden region to be bright for from one to three months'. The Lily Garden was for her primarily a spring and autumn garden, so April and May bring a proliferation of spring-flowering bulbs, pansies and wallflowers, while August and September see the flowering of hot-coloured herbaceous perennials.

The Rose and Iris Garden

The Rose and Iris Garden was originally laid out by Forbes purely as a rose garden. In 1925, at the outer elbows and in each arm of the four inner, L-shaped beds, Jekyll placed *R*. 'Blanche Double de Coubert' and *R*. 'Zéphirine Drouhin' underplanted with hybrid tea roses in four colours; the latter have now been replaced by the musk roses 'Penelope', 'Buff Beauty', 'Cornelia' and 'Felicia'. Jekyll also added intricacy and interest to the outer borders by planting bold evergreen shrubs, together with herbs, herbaceous perennials and a selection of

bearded irises in every shade then available. The garden is enclosed by brick walling on two sides and box hedging on the other two; outside on the east hedge, a fine basket-weave brick path leads along the Lavender Walk through a wooden gate hung with *Hydrangea petiolaris* to an oak bridge spanning the moat. Here in a long rectangle are two mounded beds filled with tall herbaceous perennials, with a hint of rusticity given by handmade hazel tripods. There were originally four beds, which continued across the front of the Buss Stalls used for rearing veal calves; the number of beds was halved when the handsome pergola opposite was built in 1980 and surrounded by plants to extend the season of interest.

The White Garden

The White Garden retains Forbes' geometrical 1920s layout of concentric circles within a square; at its heart is the statue of a dancing faun, originally brought from the Lyles' former home, Beel House.

Jekyll's original planting scheme of roses, peonies and irises was swept away in 1986 when the roses grew tired. It was redesigned by Andrew Lyle and head gardener Christine Brain with a nod to Sissinghurst but also a bow to Jekyll, who had praised white gardens in her book, *Colour in the Flower Garden*, and had drawn up white schemes for the Strode inner courtyard that were never implemented.

A great number and variety of carefully chosen plants climb, strike a pose, froth and loll in relaxed Edwardian exuberance. In the outer borders *Crambe cordifolia, Lysimachia ephemerum*, and *Campanula lactiflora* 'Alba' occupy the background, with white and cream sweet peas and *Solanum jasminoides* 'Album' on twiggy tripods marking the corners, and hostas, helichrysum and iberis, white arabis, and *Viola septentrionalis* as front edging. Sunny beds have *Lychnis coronaria* 'Alba' and *Verbascum chaixii* 'Album', shady beds *Dicentra spectabilis* 'Alba' and *Polygonatum biflorum*. White irises are planted in the back beds.

In spring one wall is blanketed by the long and delicate racemes of white wisteria, followed on the east wall by climbing white roses, 'Iceberg' and 'White Cockade'. Other Jekyll trademarks abound: arabis, stachys, gypsophila, aquilegias and white myosotis. The effect is indeed very white, although a few rogue colours, particularly from the ubiquitous tulips, are encouraged to stray in.

'No pampas grass and no monkey puzzles'

Andrew Lyle

Gertrude Jekyll

Gertrude Jekyll wrote more than a decade before her involvement at Barrington: 'I am growing old and tired, and suffer from very bad and painful sight. My garden is my workshop, my place of study and place of rest.' Her work for Arthur Lyle, described by her biographer Richard Bisgrove as 'inventively geometrical, embodying the finest traditions of the builder's craft in walls, steps, pools and other constructions, but furnished with a subtly woven tapestry of planting which enhanced without obscuring the design', showed that old age and increasing blindness had dimmed little of her genius. Her collaboration with Forbes was almost as fruitful as her relationship with the architect Edwin Lutyens. With her dislike of rich people who gardened only through 'hirelings', Gertrude would have approved of the keen and knowledgeable gardener Elsie Lyle and shared with Arthur a love of collecting (in her case, old tools).

The White Garden
in July

The Kitchen Garden

Conceived by Colonel Lyle and built by J.E. Forbes as an essential part of the model estate, it is perhaps surprising that Gertrude Jekyll had no hand in it. It is that rarity: a surviving and – more importantly still – thriving example of the genre.

Decorative and productive

Unlike many of those created in earlier centuries, it was not located miles from the house, but within a short walking distance. Lying diagonally opposite the formal flower gardens and separated from them only by a narrow path, the layout of these two walled enclosures is remarkably similar: both are introduced by very broad herbaceous borders planted in front; both are entered through a decorative arch; both are backed on one side by buildings; both occupy about an acre; both are divided into four unequal spaces intersected by crossing paths. It is tempting to think of them as the two faces of gardening: the decorative and the productive.

The erection of the locally quarried stone walls, topped by tiled ridges and pierced by arched gateways, was the Colonel's first building project. Started in 1921, the garden has been in continuous production ever since. On either side of the main Kitchen Garden are two narrow rectangles. The first is occupied by a glasshouse, five cold frames and a potting shed, but the attractive little building on its western wall is a racquets court, built with dormers instead of interior lighting to the specification of Arthur Lyle, a keen player. In the second, a pair of arches leads through to a cucumber pit, the original boiler house and a gardeners' store.

An allotment of gardeners
There has been a wonderful continuity of head gardeners at Barrington since 1920: only four in all, with two of them serving 27 and 28 years, and the present incumbent currently 39, and counting.

A feast of plenty

The main vista through the archway, of a copper beech hedge focusing on a lily pond dominated by a statue, *Boy with a Swan*, gives no hint of the almost industrial scale of the produce to come. Row upon row of legumes and salads, potatoes, brassicas, asparagus, sea kale, globe artichokes, cardoons (a relative of the globe artichoke), peas and beans, marrows and courgettes, leeks and parsnips are rotated in a four-yearly cycle. Originally all of the garden produce would have been consumed by the household; today visitors to the restaurant are the lucky recipients, and what isn't used there is available in the shop. The vegetable plots are raised above the level of the paths, their soil retained by blocks of rough local stone. Hand weeding has given way to mechanisation and disease-resistant varieties are chosen to cut down on spraying. The central borders are filled with flowers for cutting, and the enclosing walls drip with apples and pears, peaches, nectarines and apricots, plums, gages and damsons, figs, cherries and grapes. The kitchen garden year is an unending cycle of production and consumption, remarkable to see on such a scale.

Left The view towards the Kitchen Garden focuses on a pair of statues, *Boy with a Swan* (foreground) and *Achilles* (background)

Above right Lettuces and salad leaves fill the beds and service the restaurant

Right Decorative meets productive in June, with sweet Williams and cardoons fringing the paths and espalier and cordon pears on the east-facing wall

The Orchards

Orchards still embrace the Court on three sides. The Front Orchard lies off the main path leading to the entrance front, Goose Orchard immediately south of the Kitchen Garden, and East Orchard east of the Court.

The latter had its role redefined by Sir Ian Lyle, who in 1950 planted the pleached red-twigged Lime Walk to form a central vista from the Court, following this with an arboretum started in 1967. In spring there are about 450 apple trees in blossom, many of them underplanted with daffodils. The grass is cut in July – substitute the motor mower for the scythe, and the scene could be an illustration in a medieval Book of Hours.

A long tradition

In the 17th century, however, the house was virtually embowered in apple trees, for a very good reason. As recorded by traveller, Celia Fiennes in 1696: 'In most parts of Sommersetshire it is very fruitful for orchards… many apples and peares.' Cider-making has long been an important part of the Court's economy, and since its centenary in 2007 Barrington has been producing award-winning dry and medium ciders and apple juices from the 10 acres of trees in the grounds, together with another 10 acres further afield.

The very names of the apples are lip-smacking. Here are over 100 different varieties, mostly local and heritage in origin, ranging from the genteel 'Kingston Black', 'Newton Wonder' and 'Tom Putt' (a big red apple named after a local lord of the manor), to the wisecracking

'Hen's Turd', 'Sheep's Nose' and 'Slack ma Girdle'. Culinary and especially dessert apples are used for apple juice and are picked by hand; the dryer varieties, which are allowed to fall to the ground and are then collected by hand, go to make cider. They are crushed on a 200-year-old cider press, and the cider is sold at Barrington and in other National Trust shops.

Above 'Yarlington Mill' apples – a local cider variety

Left Goose Orchard

Gates and statues

Arthur Lyle did not confine himself to the interiors of the buildings at Barrington. All around the estate and within the gardens are eye-catching features that are appropriately large in scale. Gates were either bought or especially made to fit particular spaces – the two facing each other on the South Lawn have ornate filigree work of a very high order, while in the Kitchen Garden the wrought-iron grille is topped by an oval. The

ironwork grilles were made by Singers of Frome and other gates were the work of a local blacksmith. Many of the lead cisterns and statues – *Achilles, four dolphins,* the *Boy with a Swan* – came from Crowthers of London, who are still in business today.

A Working Estate

Under the Lyles the number of estate workers mirrored the grand days of the Daubeneys.

During the 1920–25 restoration, 103 people were employed at the Court. Even after the building work was completed, quite apart from the domestic staff, there were farm managers and farm workers, gamekeepers, gardeners, carpenters, laundrymaids, chauffeurs and odd-job men permanently on the payroll.

The First World War left its indelible mark on the running of the estate. The staff transport was an old ambulance driven by Charlie Bowdrey, who had served in the Middlesex Regiment, one of those to have incurred the heaviest losses. Men returning from the trenches were regularly employed as labourers on the restoration work. One of them, Alfred Cornelius, who worked on converting Strode House and also laid some of the decorative brick paths in the formal gardens, was landlord of the Royal Oak in the village; at lunchtime he used to line up glasses of beer on the bar for the Court workers. During the Second World War, the gardening staff were mostly in the Home Guard, and sometimes made unfortunate errors, including setting fire to the whole length of a shrubbery when practising with Molotov cocktails. Military style parades, held on the terrace of the Lily Garden, marked Saturday morning paydays.

Barrington's Captain

Above all, there was the splendidly moustachioed Captain Beacham, OBE, DSC, MC, who held the reins at Barrington for 40 years. The most gallant of soldiers, he was RSM of all three battalions of the Coldstream Guards, was mentioned for bravery in dispatches four times, and rose through the ranks through promotions in the field to become Lieutenant Colonel – reverting to Captain when he joined the staff as estate manager in 1921, so as not to outrank his employer. Beacham was with Arthur Lyle when he died aboard ship on his way to the West Indies in 1931 and helped supervise his colonel's burial at sea.

Far left Alfred Cornelius, pictured with his granddaughters Jean and June in 1936

Left The 21-year-old Lieutenant Arthur Lyle, set to join the second Boer War in South Africa

Batting Beacham

Betty Beacham was at least as formidable as her father. She played cricket at national level, scoring 50 against the Australians at Trent Bridge in 1951. Watching village boys re-enacting the latest Test match one summer's day in 1957, she leapt forward to take a fine catch low down on the left-hand side. Village protocol dictated that she be invited to bat, and she proceeded to hit the youthful star bowler's ball all over the ground before retiring.

'Beacham marched everywhere, preceded by whiffs of strong pipe tobacco,' recalls Andrew Lyle. The great transfer of the Colonel's panelling and wooden artefacts from Amersham to Barrington, which involved a fleet of lorries and took three weeks to accomplish, was masterminded by Beacham as a military manoeuvre. The estate staff deferred to him, the evacuee schoolboys were terrified of him.

Above Colonel Lyle's agent, Robert William Beacham, with his family

Afterword

Children who grew up at Barrington during the years after the Second World War – young Lyles, sons and daughters of staff members, schoolboy evacuees – remember with nostalgia the immense sense of space surrounding the Court and the joy of roaming the fields, hills and woods on foot or by bike. No tarmac, no cars, no noise.

Today, visitors are invited to explore, and if you can spare the time, it's well worth making the effort to stroll through the park, meadows, farmland and lanes that surround the Court and make up its beautiful backdrop.

Now a contemporary part of the village and local community, the landscape, estate and outbuildings continue to be managed. Traditional skills have been re-created, and the house and garden resound once again with companionable activity. Fruit and vegetables are harvested from the Kitchen Garden and dances are held in the Great Hall. The only change is that it is no longer the Lyle family who bring life and purpose to the place, but our visitors, staff and volunteers.

Above Visitors, glimpsed through Lutyens Gate from Goose Orchard, explore the walled flower gardens

Right Children gathering fallen apples for cider-making at Barrington's annual Apple Day